1 *Billy Hunkin sitting on a gurry.* Valentine.

'Now when I lived Downalong there was Pinhooks, hooked up like a navvy's breakfast, and Ben Huggins, that was tacked on when he was a boy. Then there was Chickee Wedge, Pardn'aff, Dick Shanero, Edward La. He was always singing, a big chapel man he was and he was always tuning, la la, Edward La they called him. Wrinklow, he was a Richards. Ennie Puddie, she was always making puddings. Sally Trotters, she was always going like a mail train. Georgy Beltee, Dick Salt, his father before him was called that. Susie Buzz, she was a Pollard, her father before her was Willy Buzz, that's the name they had pinned on them. Then there was Willy Spry. His toe nails used to grow under his feet and he used to carry around a small basket with groceries in. His brother, Dick Spry, was called Shiny Eels because he used to clean the front of his shoes but not the heels. There were three sisters used to live up Street-an-Garrow who were Salvationists. Snuffs they used to call them. They was Home Leaguers like my mother. I've an old fashioned photograph of her with the Home Leaguers but its gone yella with age.

Then there was Flap, she used to do the marinated pilchards. Berryman her name was and she lived in Bunkers Hill. Freddy Whisper, he was a Grenfell. His father before him was called Whisper as he used to talk so very low. His son used to hollar like the devil, but they called him Whisper. I think he had something wrong with his hooverlaw, larynx, foofoo valve. Then there was Slippery. His grandfather was always afraid he was going to slip down. I used to know the old man and he used to be all green with the seaweed down there. Now Carganawl and Pollawosses wife were two sisters. Anthony Taddely. He used to have the Bakehouse down there where the Betting shop is now in behind Barber the Barber. Markee, he was a Trevorrow. He was a Bible Christian and there used to be a little crew of them that used to sit one side of the chapel, The Old Saints' they used to call them, they used to say "Here, Markee's coming." Beautiful singers they were. There was goodness in chapel then.

'Then there was Lively, he used to live in the old arch. He used to walk so very swift that they called him Lively, really he was too slow to catch a cold. Shilloff was his son. He would always ask for a drink with the chill off. Then there's High George. He used to live down Church Place and he had false teeth that would never fit. He'd always hold his head up high. His false teeth were always dropping, so they called him High George. Franky Ivy. We used to go and ask Franky Ivy to tell us our fortune. He used to tell fortunes in the cards. Then there's Franky Flip, his real name was Franky Nichols but lots of people would call him Town Bull. He was a smart man with a high topper hat on and squirty tails. Then there was Anny Duck. She always used to wear shoes with the heels trowled over, one was looking towards Hellesveor moors and the other one was looking towards Nancecoot.'

2 *Pilchard Boats from Smeaton's pier.* Frith.

A St. Ives Album

ANDREW LANYON

3 *St. Ives from the grounds of Tregenna Castle.*   *c.* 1900. Comley.

Alison Hodge

First published in 1979 by
Alison Hodge, 5 Chapel Street, Penzance, Cornwall
Reprinted 1979.
© *Andrew Lanyon, 1979*

ISBN 0 906 720 00 1
Design and Origination by TNR Productions Ltd., London.

Produced by Dowrick Design and Print, St. Ives, Cornwall.

Acknowledgements: The author and publisher would like to thank the
following for their kind permission to reproduce photographs: Percy
Quick, nos. 1,4,5,28,36,37,42,47,58,59,60,79,80,82 and back cover. Truro
Museum, nos. 13,14,22,23,31,38,39,40,41,50,61,62,64,65,67,76,86,91. St.
Ives Museum, nos. 17,52,85; Harold C. Franklin, nos. 9,49 and 81. H.C.
Comley, nos. 32 and 57. W.H. Paynter, no. 27. Cyril Honey, no. 92. All other
photographs belong to the author.

4 *The 'New' or 'Wooden' pier in about 1870, six years after it
was begun and only a year or so before it began to break up.*

Front cover: *the boy on the left is Mathee Paraffin (Stevens) who was
later a mason. He lived at Wheal Dream and had a granny called Alice
who kept a china shop and wore long dresses. Boys used to go in and say,
'Mother do like that ther pot', pointing to one at the back, and she would
sweep towards it in her long dress knocking over all the china.*

These were 'Downalong' boys, a race apart from those that lived
'Upalong'. The border was the market house, near the church, and
the two sides would clash if either wandered into the other's
territory. If Upalong or 'Sanders Lane' boys came beyond the
market house there would be 'broom hilts and cudgels flying'.

The boats in the picture are 'tinnen' boats, made from Sharp's
toffee tins, bent over at the ends and flattened with a stone. They
were filled with sand for ballast and had a paper or cloth sail. A
matchbox became a wheelhouse and sometimes they had real
fires going. Mathee Paraffin's boat is up on the rocks probably
because it was leaky. Boys would push their 'tinnen' boats
through the sand in the harbour then exclaim, 'Es no fish here, I'm
goin to the North Sea' and take them round to Porthmeor.
*c.*1900   Douglas.

Back cover: *the harbour in the 1880s.*   Ashton.

5 *The market place before the demolition in 1887 of the fifteenth-century inn the George and Dragon (to left of centre).*

'After visiting Providence mine, and having a long chat with that intelligent and amiable old patriarch, Captain John Anthony, he arrived, about three o'clock, very sore and very hungry, "at the town that went down on the sea-shore to get washed, and hadn't the strength to get back again." After satisfying his stomach with a splendid fish dinner and other good things, readily served at the "Western" Hotel, he sallied out to view the new pier, of which the men of St. Ives are so proud. From seeing many quaint, picturesque old houses around the Market place, he was induced to wander through the labyrinth of alleys and lanes into the back settlements, hoping to find some structure ancient enough to pass for the habitation of the mythical personage of the seven wives. He found some dwellings which he thought (reasonably enough) must have been built before Noah's time, when it might have been thoroughly washed, but the traveller did not think it could ever have been cleansed since, from the sickening smells, and stunning odours of the very essence of stench, which saluted him at every turn, as he picked his way through the Dijey, and leaped the gutters about Charn Chy. It was in the midst of a busy fishery season, and he saw enough, and smelt too much, to satisfy his curiosity, without proceeding any further quayward. As soon as he got back to the "Western", he fortified his rebellious stomach (that now detested fish) with good store of Mr. Hodge's best brandy. Then he was got on board his nag, and took his course up the Stennack, intending to return to Penzance by the old road and examine the works and machinery at Wheal Reeth mine on the way.'

William Bottrell ʻTRADITIONS AND HEARTHSIDE STORIESʼ

This description by William Bottrell of a Birmingham pinmaker's visit to St. Ives in the mid-1870s, conveys something of the flavour of the town in its heyday. At about the same date a more illustrious visitor, the Reverend Francis Kilvert, noted in his diary,[1] 'The vicar of St. Ives says the stench there is so terrific as to stop the church clock.' However, it was not the clock that stopped, but the fish, and only a few decades later fishing began to decline and sail lofts were converted into artists' studios.

From the time Turner sketched the view across the Bay, painters began to flood into St. Ives in such numbers that the place must have started to smell of turpentine. Gradually scenery replaced fish in importance, and the huge fleets that had once sailed in and out of the harbour were blown across an easel sea. In the wake of the painters, largely as a result of the railway reaching St. Ives, the seasonal flow of visitors began to create a new rhythm. Hard on the heels of these first tourists came the view merchants, representatives of firms like Valentine and Frith, whose cameras broke off bits of old St. Ives, disgorging them as penny postcards. As this new creature, the photographer, emerged to focus a shining eye on St. Ives, so the *plein air* painter took off his Norfolk jacket and went indoors.

St. Ives now became tidy and comfortable enough to encourage visitors to stay, while retaining some of the charm that brought them. In fact St. Ives has managed with some success to withstand the forces that begin to destroy a place as soon as is decided to preserve it. As long ago as 1892 J.H. Matthews[2] observed, 'the old narrow, crooked, ill-paved streets still charm the artistic eye and shock the olfactory nerves.' Today, after nearly ninety years of creeping symmetry the artistic eye still finds something attractive. 'A typical St. Ives house', wrote Matthews, 'is peculiar for the convenient irregularity of its plan of construction, and for the snug solidity of the structure.' Yet however solid the structure, bits gradually fall down or are knocked off and so the irregularities are smoothed out, until one day we shall have only the paintings and these photographs to remind us of a time when St. Ives functioned in the manner for which she was built.

1. *Kilvert's Diary*. Cape 1944, Penguin 1977.
2. J.H. Matthews, *History of St. Ives*, Elliot Stock 1892.

6 *John Douglas, a double-exposure self portrait.*

John Douglas and Edward Ashton were two among the many photographers who were consistently successful in catching St. Ives at a time when the 'malodorous atmosphere' still clung to her. Unfortunately identification of many of their photographs is not always possible, because Douglas's negatives became mixed with Herbert Lanyon's and the majority of Ashton's photographs exist only as unsigned prints. There are more classic photographs attributable to Douglas than to Ashton, but Ashton's was probably the more unusual talent. He enjoyed building strong compositions, for example by frequently placing long lines of figures across the sand in contrast to the tall verticals of boats' masts. Such figures appear like a musical score, with the occasional isolated figure added as an exuberant trill.

If Ashton excelled at such geometric arrangements of people in scenery, similar to Alfred Wallis's later jigsawing of boats, Douglas's work is generally more romantic. He paid more attention to people, moving his camera closer and often arranging them so that their attention was directed within the picture rather than out of it, as Ashton preferred. The photograph of the two boys on the cover must be a classic, combining as it does a superb composition with clear subject matter. Douglas, with his sophisticated Upalong eye, contrasts to Ashton's more crudely fashioned pictures in which the figures seem almost wooden, but which are placed with as much care as windows in a cottage Downalong.

7 *Edward Ashton.*

8 *L.E. Comley outside his shop in Fore Street.*

9 *The harbour before the extension of Smeaton's pier in 1888. This extension, together with the widening of the wharf, created a far shallower harbour and meant boat building on the sand was no longer possible.*

Two more St. Ives photographers, L.E. Comley and W.J. Cooper, serve as examples of how fortune graces the work of some, while that of others is lost almost without trace. Although the majority of Comley's quarter-and half-plate negatives have survived intact, practically all Cooper's work has been destroyed. His negatives were wiped clean and the glass re-used during the war, and those prints that were not pulped went up in flames. Cooper was an amateur taxidermist as well as photographer and a relative who remembers doing 'toning for a penny' as a child also remembers the bonfire that claimed numerous photographs and stuffed birds.

Comley ran a draper's shop, but was also a very successful amateur photographer whose pictures were bought up by a variety of postcard firms for reproduction. His son, Mr. H.C. Comley, frequently accompanied him as assistant and remembers how on windy days they would have to anchor the tripod to the ground. He also remembers his father discussing photography with John Douglas, the subject invariably being the merits of soft romantic pictures versus those of sharp outlines and crisp detail. Comley was of the latter school and preferred to cover events rather as a reporter, intent on capturing a scene as it happened. Douglas, being of the more 'misty moody' school preferred when possible to arrange his figures carefully.

Many of the following photographs show signs of age, either through deterioration of a print, or more usually by the cracking of a glass negative. The emulsion of the original glass plate of these pilot boats being built in the harbour has crazed, adding its own nostalgia, like ivy on a ruin, and reminding us of the century that separates us from this scene.

10,11 *Hauling a seine boat up on to Porthminster.* *c.* 1900. Comley.

12 *The harbour filled with the clutter of a busy fishing port.*

c. 1900. Comley.

13 *A breezy summer view of St. Ives from Porthminster.*

1903. Hughes.

14 *A less tranquil view. The wreck of the steamship* Rosedale *after a terrific storm in which the whole bay became a seething mass of foam, and in which three other boats, the* Cintra, Bessie *and* Vulture *were wrecked in Carbis Bay. During the night both the rocket apparatus and the lifeboat were skillfully deployed in saving lives. The* Rosedale *eventually had to be demolished with explosives, bits of the hull apparently falling all over St. Ives. Although one of the demolition men claimed that certain pieces of metal went up in the sky and 'were never seen no more', one man remembers being fascinated and somewhat puzzled as a child by a curious keel-shaped piece of iron embedded in one of the seine boats on Porthminster.*

November 1893. Hughes.

15 *This 'Cornish Giant' was photographed at St. Ives by Herbert Lanyon, whose camera was washed off the rocks seconds later.*

16 *Self portrait by Herbert Lanyon, musician, traveller and amateur photographer.*

17 *The lifeboat* Covent Garden, c. 1874. *This was the second R.N.L.I. lifeboat to be stationed at St. Ives. Adams, a local boatbuilder, had designed and built the first one in 1840. The* Covent Garden *had a noble record of service. On 2 February, 1873 she was launched five times in a single day, exhausting five crews but saving thirteen men off three vessels shipwrecked at St. Ives during a violent storm.*

18 *The last of the sail lifeboats, the* James Stevens. Comley.

19 *Elizabeth and William Barber in Pudding Bag Lane, so called because it was 'in one way out the same'. The wooden bins were used for storing coal while the wash 'troys' came in useful during the Regatta.*
                                                                    c. 1900. Douglas.

20 *St. Ives Regatta.*   *c.* 1900. Comley.

21 *Mending a net in a sail loft.*   *c.* 1900. Comley.

c. 1890. Ashton.

22 *Barnoon Hill. This view, together with the 'Old Arch', was one of the most photographed in St. Ives, itself probably one of the most photographed of places at this time.*

BARNOON·HILL

c. 1890. Ashton.

23 *Slates and cement-wash, brick, granite and cobblestones combine to produce a wealth of textures in this view from Ayr Lane.*

24 *Gutting ling and putting them in a barrel with salt.*

1890s. Valentine.

25 *Scalding a pig prior to scraping off the bristles. Douglas recomposed this scene from a larger view and also reversed it.*   *c.* 1900. Douglas.

26 *Early geometry lesson on the sand.* *c.* 1900. Douglas.

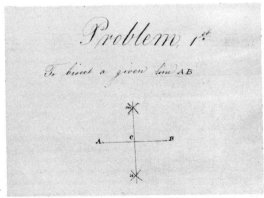

27 *Page from a child's school book.*

28 *Playing marbles beside a trading vessel in the harbour at St. Ives.* *c.* 1890. Ashton?

The game was called 'Rings'. A ring was made in the sand and each player placed several marbles in it; any he knocked out he kept. R.P. Bennetts ('Sligs') is the man playing the marble; above him to the left stands Philip Noall ('Sparrow Hawk') and behind Noall to the right is a Telegraph boy. This was perhaps any day but a Sunday, since 'if you went on the beach on a Sunday you'd make sure you got the sand off your shoes.' In his *History of St. Ives,* Matthews notes that, 'Some time in the 1860s a mayor of St. Ives had a young man put in the stocks for playing marbles on Good Friday.' (J.H. Matthews, History of St. Ives, 1892.) When the weather was bad the men used to play in the chapel where the knuckle hold can still be seen. Anyone who succeeded in rolling his marble into the 'nekky ole' got his knuckle down behind it and flicked it out at the marbles around.

29 *One-eyed William Barber who lived in Pudding Bag Lane. When he retired from fishing he supplied Downalong children with boats and Joanies (wooden dolls) carved from old oar handles.* *c.* 1900. Douglas.

30 *William Barber holding the gaff with which the shark in the photograph was caught from a rowing boat in the harbour.*
c. 1902. Comley.

31 *Then to the delight of everyone the fiddler mounted the parapet, Mr. Hawke and one of the widows followed suit, and to the Furry tune they began the time-honoured dance, the children following.'* (CORNISHMAN, 27 July, 1911.)

The celebration in memory of John Knill, collector of customs at St.Ives, was first held in 1801. His steeple, intended as his mausoleum, was designed as a landmark for sailors, but also served as a guide for smugglers.

32 *'At the top of the hill conveyances were provided which spared the members of the procession the fatiguing climb to the pyramid.'* (CORNISHMAN, 27 July, 1911.) Comley.

33 *'Here was an enormous concourse of people, estimated at 4,000, all very hot and dusty from their scramble up the hill, while settling on everyone in a fine brown powder was the dust from the turf pathway, stirred up by the passing of countless feet.'* (CORNISHMAN, 27 July, 1911.)

Knill's Monument, Festival Day, St. Ives

34 *A dancing bear such as this was usually trained on hot bricks, music being gradually introduced to fit the creature's antics. A law had recently been passed regarding the muzzling of performing animals.* 1890s. Ashton.

35 *Circus elephants being taken to romp and bathe on Porthmeor beach.* Chy an Chy, through which they are passing, means literally 'the house by the house' and possibly refers to the remote time when St. Ives was made up of only a few houses. *c.* 1900. Douglas.

36 *Mending the seine net on the Island.*
The netting of which the seine was made was called 'Dungarvan'.
According to J.H. Matthews, an Irish farmer (probably from
Dungarvan) called Stephens was shipwrecked near Zennor in
1470 with a cargo of cattle which he and two other men, Quick and
Mitchell, were bringing over from Ireland. They settled in the
parishes of Zennor and Towednack and are credited with the
introduction of seine fishing. But 'the Quicks and Mitchells, who
are also now very numerous about St. Ives', (1892) 'aver that
Stephens was only a subordinate to their own ancestors. Their
ancestors, they say, owned the cattle, and Stephens was the
drover.'   1890s. Ashton?

37 *A group of St. Ives 'beatsters' or net menders, holding their bone net
needles. Through constant attention some seine nets continued in use for
a hundred years or more.*   1890s. Ashton?

38 *The barkhouse on the Island.*   1890s. Ashton.

The men are overhauling the nets before passing them through the window of the barkhouse and into the hot vats. Without the protection of barking, the cotton nets would soon have rotted in the sea water. Bark is extracted from the bark of a tree, originally oak. Large fishing boats that worked away from their own ports, had their own barking tanks on board.

39, 40, 41 *Breaking up a large boulder in a field at Halsecommon.* There was quite an art to breaking up a stone such as this. The iron bars or 'jumpers', with their characteristic round weights, can be seen leaning against the hedge on the left. They were held with both hands, lifted not too high and turned then dropped on the same point on the rock over and over again. When a large enough hole had been made, two pieces of flat iron called 'feathers' were inserted and a chisel driven between them. Softer stone was broken with a hammer, but hard granite like this had to be jumped. Blue-stone was 'burnt' by piling wood into a trench around the stone then setting it alight. When water was thrown over the hot boulder it cracked. This specimen was probably being broken up for building the reservoir.

42 *Charley Paynter.* He was a blind poet, newsvendor, town crier and seller of blacking for shoes. According to one source he was the most unlikely person to have been town crier, for not only would he 'cough a bit then say in a very flat voice "blackin, blackin" – but he never had no bell.' But maybe he never needed a bell for close behind him is what might be a pressing-stone (for weighting fish packed in barrels to squeeze out the oil), which as J.H. Matthews tells us made its own commotion. 'When not in use, the pressing-stones are piled on the floors of the cellars or in corners of the streets. It is common superstition at St. Ives that the advent of a good shoal of pilchards is presaged by a supernatural commotion among these stones, which are then supposed to roll about spontaneously.'

43 *An art school.* *c.* 1900. Douglas.

44 *A painter, probably Julius Olsson, in his studio overlooking Porthmeor.*

c. 1900. Douglas.

He was a daring yachtsman but better known for his moonlit seas. He probably never forgave the critic who called his seascapes 'Neapolitan ices', as perhaps his fellow painter, Louis Grier, never forgave those who whispered Downalong that he painted by the mile and cut off at the yard.

45 *'We used to go down on the sand and pick up gaes, pieces of china, and we used to play fivestones, marbles, rounders, whiptops, go from St. Ives to Trelyon with hoops, scattin the 'oops with a stick, and then we used to play nella. We used to go down in the gurries, down old Tilda's cellar, down in Back Lane, and of course Downalong where I used to live.'* Betty Ralph.   c. 1900. Douglas.

46 *Two of the numerous cats that thronged the back alleys and lanes.*   *c.* 1900. Douglas.

Apparently taken about 1888-1890 when Quay was extended to 2nd flight of the arches were then built into the old & original Quay. Note the rush for the Grove which was to remove stairs Birds.

47 *Boys fishing with hand lines off Smeaton's pier.*
The harbour they are fishing into was created by the distant 'New Pier', which became a total ruin within twenty years of being built. The tracks in the foreground were for tramming the pilchards down to the harbour master's office where they were taken away by horse and cart, thus saving considerable congestion on the pier. The boy on the left is baiting a hook, probably one of several on his line. The girl would only be allowed to watch.   1870s.

48 'In a report by Her Majesty's Inspector of Schools, *'Of the girls',* it says, *'there is good order and they are cleanly and tidy. Their needlework is very fair indeed and so far as I examined them they read and write fairly. The number of children has increased since the appointment of the new master; but it seems that education is not yet much valued by the fishermen of St. Ives who give their children so many holidays that unless some change is made it will be necessary to turn out many of this class in order to make way for a more regular set of boys.'* (WESTERN MORNING NEWS, 7 August, 1865.)

49 *A seine boat 'waiting for the tide to turn'. Many such men were paid a retainer to wait around for a shoal of pilchards to be sighted in the Bay.*
1880s. Ashton.

50 *'Tucking' in progress in the Bay.*

When the tense and silent process of encircling the shoal and shooting the seine net had been accomplished, the catch was pulled into shallower waters by means of ropes or 'warps' sent ashore and fastened to capstans. These were manned by 'blowsers', who had to proceed carefully so as to edge the net into a position where the catch was in shallow enough water to allow the fish to be cleared and yet deep enough, at all states of the tide, to keep the fish alive. The next stage involved small boats called 'dippers' that shot 'tuck' nets into the larger seine net. With these, portions of the catch were cut off and raised to the surface, then scooped out with 'whiskets' (baskets). Boats were raised out of the water and placed across the dipper boats so as to balance the line of men working along one side. As soon as the men were waist high in pilchards they pulled for shore. This often continued for several days until the seine was emptied.

51 *Alfred Wallis's marine stores on the wharf.*

'In 1890, aged thirty-five, Alfred Wallis moved across the Penwith peninsula from Penzance to St. Ives, to set himself up as a marine scrap merchant. He was greatly helped by his wife, who kept the store while he went out with pony and cart collecting rags and bones. For a few years he probably continued to fish out of St. Ives, and he may well have been engaged in the seine fishing, but soon his new job took up all his time.

'The business prospered, so that in 1912 he was able to retire with adequate savings and buy his own house at 3, Back Road West. He was then only fifty-six, but Susan was seventy-seven; in any case the St. Ives fishing industry was declining rapidly, partly because the rich shoals of pilchards had disappeared.' (Arts Council catalogue for a Tate Gallery show of paintings by Alfred Wallis in 1968.)   *c.* 1910. Douglas.

A painter is at work where Wallis later had his marine stores, while a man who might be Wallis (second from right) poses for the camera among the boats that were soon to disappear for ever. It was after his wife's death in 1922 that Wallis turned to painting, an activity perhaps stimulated by the presence of so many people painting the moods of a sea Wallis felt he knew better.

'Alfred used to do his painting on cardboard and the leaves of "mogany" tables and his wife used to sing "Gospel Bells". He used to do the lighthouse in the sea and the hotel on top and the women coming down with their motoring veils on. He couldn't draw but if he was living now he'd be worth thousands of pounds because his paintings are selling like the devil.' (Betty Ralph.)

In a letter about his pictures Wallis wrote, *'i do most what used To Be what we shall never see no more as everything is altered.'*　　c. 1890. Ashton.

52 *An earlier, 1890s photograph, taken from almost the same viewpoint on the wharf.*

53 *Wallis in a Salvation Army group.*

54 *Ephraim Perkin.*   *c.* 1900. Douglas.

55 *The regular Cornish fisherman is engaged in fishing nearly all the year round, on various parts of the English and Irish coast, from the early mackerel time in January or February, to the disappearance of the pilchards in November; and these men have been described as "the hardiest and most adventurous" fishermen afloat.'* (Tregellas, TOURIST GUIDE TO CORNWALL, 1895.)   *c.* 1900. Douglas.

56 *The huers' hut overlooking St. Ives Bay.*
Also known as the 'bocking house', the huers' hut was one of many built on cliff tops around the Cornish coast from which, during the autumn, a constant lookout was kept for the characteristic reddy-brown patches in the sea that marked the presence of a shoal of pilchards. *c.* 1900. Comley.

57 *Huers directed the seine boat with 'bushes'.*
These consisted of wooden frames covered in a suitably coloured material to show up against the background of sky or building. In some coves actual furze bushes were used, hence the term. The huer waved them like semaphore flags so as to direct the boats around the constantly expanding and contracting shoal. As soon as they were in position he dropped the bushes and gave the signal through his trumpet to 'shoot the seine'.
c. 1900.   Comley.

58 *'Women and children were waiting in the cellars to begin work when the fish arrived. Each gurry, as it came, was emptied on the ground. A man stood by the heap of pilchards, and scooped them up into baskets which were carried by the children to the twenty or thirty women by the wall of the cellar. The women took the pilchards from the children and laid them down about a couple of feet from the wall, the heads pointing outwards. In the space next to the wall they were placed longways. As soon as a row of pilchards was laid down it was covered with salt, and the pile went on increasing in alternate layers of fish and salt, until it was as high as the women could conveniently reach. This process was known as 'bulking'. The bulks were left for three or four weeks, when the fish were considered to be cured.'*
(William Paynter, OLD ST. IVES.)   1871. Ashton?

59 *Unloading fish into gurries.*

60 *'St. Ives Flooded. Enormous Damage. Miraculous Escapees. Never in its history has St. Ives been visited by such a disaster as occurred yesterday. The main portion of the town has been literally swamped, buildings damaged, roads torn up, and families have been dislodged from their houses to view their furniture floating down through a torrent of water into the lower parts of the town.... It is presumed that by some means or other the river got choked, probably from the tremendous rush of water which came down it. Certain it is that a perfect torrent broke away from half way up the Stennack close by Umfula-place, and poured with a loud roar down the main streets.'* (WESTERN MORNING NEWS, 13 November, 1894.)

61 *Water pouring down towards the station from above the Malakoff.*

62 *A view down Tregenna Hill.*

St. Ives.

After the Flood.

Hodge, Stationer, St. Ives.

63 *The force of the flood had been so terrific that huge rocks and stones were carried into the lower streets.*

64 *The launching of the* Unity *on Porthgwidden beach.*

The *Unity* was probably built by the Trevorrows, a well-known family of boat builders at Porthgwidden. When a boat was launched in this fashion the Shanty man would sing out 'Orensheboree', and as the men took the strain the boat would slide down the greased skids into the water. Sadly, five years later, on 2 December, 1893, the *Evening Tidings* reported, *The fishing boat* Unity, *a 35' craft, owned and captained by Mr. William Cattran of Mousehole, went down this morning, early, off Lamorna. The* Unity *left Newlyn pier yesterday afternoon to go to Mullion for herrings and having been loaded she started again for Newlyn. On the way up the wind freshened considerably, and when off Lamorna the* Unity, *which was very heavily laden, sank. The crew, consisting of the captain and three men, took to the small boat. Two of them landed, and the other two pulled to Mousehole.'*   1888. Ashton.

65 *The German brig* Albert Wilhelm, *bound for Fowey in ballast, wrecked in a storm on Porthquidnack beach. No lives were lost but the owner suffered a great loss as the vessel was insured for only £45.*

The weather moderated considerably yesterday, and a number of persons visited the wreck. It presented a mournful spectacle. Only one mast was standing, the main mast having fallen overboard shortly after she struck. A small piece of the shattered mast remained standing, the remainder was lying on the beach, connected with the vessel by the entangled gear. She was lying broadside on to the beach, and the depth she was embedded in the sand shewed the terrible force with which she must have been tossed about by the storm. There is not the slightest hope of her being saved, and the work of stripping her was accordingly being vigorously carried out yesterday while the tide permitted. (WESTERN MORNING NEWS, 18 October, 1886.)

Ashton.

66 *Making crab and lobster-pots.*   *c.* 1900. Comley.

67 *The harbour before the extension of Smeaton's pier in 1888, with Ashton's characteristically grouped figures.*

68 *A scyther inland from St. Ives.*
Stiff corduroy trousers were customarily soaked in horse urine to soften them and increase their wearing quality. The straight-shanked west country scythe is used with a sort of tugging motion, not the sweep associated with the normal curved shank.

69 *Sharpening the blade.*   *c.* 1900. Douglas.

70 *Backs of the Warren houses during a gale.*

c. 1910. Lanyon.

71 *'On Tuesday night the wind flew round to the north and blew with hurricane force. Our St. Ives correspondent telegraphing late last night states that a terrific gale was blowing at St. Ives, and that the three-masted schooner* Lizzie R. Wilce *is ashore on Porthminster beach. The crew of five were saved by the St. Ives lifeboat. As we go to press we hear that another schooner has been wrecked on Porthminster beach this morning.*

(CORNISHMAN, 9 January, 1908.)

The second schooner was the *Mary Barrow* and her crew of five was also taken off by the lifeboat.   1908. Comley.

72 *The same scene from the harbour side.*   Comley.

73 *The fish hanging out to dry is a ray, of which in 1662 the naturalist Ray wrote, 'The people of Brittany drive a great trade here for* raiae, *which they dry in the sun, and then carry away. In exchange for this they bring salt.'*

In the Digey, St. Ives   Valentines Series

74 *Old Paddy and Margaret Flighty, as well as some pressing-stones.*

75 *A studio overlooking the harbour.* *c.* 1900. Douglas.

76 *A 'civilized' melodrama unfolds Upalong, with an occasional wooden 'thwack' on the lawn, far above the screeching gulls.* Ashton.

77 *In the harbour.*   *c.* 1900. Douglas.

78 *The usual Preaching of the Passion was less successful on the Wharf than it has been in previous years, partly owing to the large catches of Mackerel which employed so many, and the consequent frequent disturbance of the congregation by the fish carts on their way to the Railway Station, and partly owing to the unfavourable weather which at last compelled an adjournment to the Mariners Chapel. Though we regretted the frequent interruptions, yet the knowledge that the traffic would greatly benefit the poor of the Parish more than counterbalanced the regret.'* (ST. IVES PENNY POST AND MONTHLY RECORD, 1878.)   *c.* 1900. Douglas.

"When the Boats come in".   Valentines Series

79 *A popular early postcard with, in the background, the unusual and beautiful lighthouse designed in 1831 by James and Edward Harvey. This was later dwarfed by the cast-iron pepper mill at the end of the 1888 extension.*

80 *The boy with the spade is William James Hodge (Cashu) and the man (Ape) is his grandfather.*

The punt on which he is sitting belonged to the *Gratitude*, which, with a 46-foot keel was the largest St. Ives mackerel boat. In the background are stacks of fish-buyers' boxes, and a horse and cart waiting to take fish from the punts to the buyers for counting and barrelling. Above Shamrock Lodge on the right is an old gas street light. On 9 September, 1835, a meeting of the inhabitants of St. Ives was held to consider the advisability of lighting the town with gas. The motion was carried, though one man, the only one to object, expressed his contempt for the proceedings in the following verse:

> *'Tis well for us the sun and moon,*
> *Are up so very high,*
> *That no presumptuous hand can reach*
> *To pluck them from the sky.*
> *If 'twere not so, I do not doubt*
> *But some Reforming Ass*
> *Would soon propose to snuff them out,*
> *And light the world with Gas!'*

Diary of John Tregerthen Short.

81 *A cracked negative by Ashton of the harbour and opposite an example of a badly torn print.*

82 *A shop on the wharf, run by the woman in the centre, Catherine Trevorrow ('Cattern'), which sold everything from sweets and groceries to buttons and bootlaces.*
Inside the window above the steps was a day school, attended by pupils at a cost of 2d a week. The child's hoop belonged to Cattern's neice, who gave this information to Percy Quick.

83 *When 'Ol Son' Phillips retired from sailing in the tea clippers he made his living by carrying fish to and from Newlyn in his cart. The photograph shows his stables where he also kept pigs, ducks, geese and chickens. Against the wall is a packing case for paintings from Lanham and Co., who opened the first art gallery in St. Ives in 1887. The date printed on the wood and reversed in the negative is 4/12/99.*   *c.* 1900. Douglas.

84 *Driving bees in order to take out the honeycombs.*

'A fine day, when bees are flying freely, is to be preferred.... With the opening between the skeps in front of you, so that you may observe all that occurs, rap the sides of the lower skep — the sides to which the combs are attached — sharply with the palms of your hands, or with two sticks, taking care that while jarring the combs slightly you do not loose or break them down. Carry on the rapping continuously at the rate of about two per second. The bees will speedily run up past the skewer into the upper skep. Driving, whether open or closed, may usually be completed in about a quarter of an hour.' (J.G. Digges, PRACTICAL BEE GUIDE)

c. 1900. Douglas.

85 *The* General Havelock, *a mackerel boat, entering the harbour.*   *c.* 1890.

86 *Baileys Lane. Dick Ninnis giving Matthew Stevens a ride in his 'barra'. He was errand boy for the Star grocery shop.*

c. 1900. Valentine.

87 *A lovely portrait, of both child and cat, by Douglas.*

88 *A stuffed badger positioned in the undergrowth above Clodgy Point.*
This photograph was probably taken by William Cooper, a St. Ives greengrocer who often exchanged provisions for paintings by local artists, and who in this postcard has combined his two main interests, taxidermy and photography. Although only a few of Cooper's photographs survive, several of his stuffed animals have found their way into the St. Ives Museum.

89 *Seagulls photographed in the days when they nested only on the cliffs.*
Now they have moved inland, onto rooftops and occasionally even into trees. This is only one of a large number of seagull pictures by Douglas. Although it seems he was interested in them from an artistic rather than an ornithological viewpoint, the whole collection represents a valuable study of these scavengers. *c.* 1900 Douglas.

90 *Fishermen returning home. 'I remember when the herring boats were coming in and we used to go down and see them unmeshing, all the men with their leather sea boots on and coming up with all the shales.'* (Betty Ralph.)

c. 1900. Douglas.

91 *An 1860s scene, possibly the earliest surviving photograph of St. Ives.*

Then there was Tilly Toots, she wasn't a bad old stick. Then there was Joa. He was Anny Duck's husband Joa was, he used to always wear a white silk scarf round his neck and a jersey. They used to call him Jersey Frocks. Then there was Billy Bunken, he used to live in Street-an-Garrow and sharpen all the saws. And then there was Launder Lugg. He used to live in Back Lane and we used to go up and tease him and he'd take a stick and wack away if he were in our area. We used to go up and aggravate him a bit.

'Then there was Dan Rags. Now he was nicknamed that I think because he always had his trousers ripped, or his father before him and of course the name fell down. Dan Nubs, he used to live next door to Yanks. He wasn't no higher than three pence. And Walter Starling. Richards was his name. Once upon a time Tregenna Castle belonged to his father, but he couldn't read nor write, he put a cross you see and they gave him a bit of money for it. He was called Walter Starling, because he was always chirpin' like a bird. Billy Bluenose, even his dustbin he used to paint blue as basam. Everything he had was blue. Dick Worm was always catching worms. Then there was Lizzie Coalbags. She's the one that went in my house in Trelawney Road. This is the bungalow that her mother left that I'm in now. The walls was rotten with the nails from the Christmas decorations. I pulled out sixteen thousand seven hundred tacks.

'Then there was Robby Hight, his name was Wedge and he was coxswain of the lifeboat once. Stewed Mackie, he used to live up at Ayr. Then there was George Appeye and Myonny. Then there's My John, he's the man used to make herby beer. He used to pick herbs from the hedges and if you weren't careful how you took the cork off you'd go up the ceiling, cork and all. Then there was Pint an a Pennerd. He got that name because he would drink some and then ask for a pennerd, a pennyworth see. Pint an a Pennerd. Then there's Dashin Billows. He had great big teeth. Poor old devil, he used to have fits awful. I've seen him fall down on the wharf down there and he never marked himself. There was Mickey Tinsy, Hookanasha, Willy Blackdog, Jack Farl, Jimmy Stingbum, Jemmy Lempotts, Dick Salt, Merly, Curly, Hatty Edwards, Georgy Trowl, Mary Ann Clemm, Bessie Two Thumbs, Mary Wisdom, Bessie Pork'n Greens, Dick Fing, John Dykes, Willy Unchy and then there's Yanks, but they've all passed on now. That's all that I remember when I lived Downalong.'   (Betty Ralph)

92 *Betty Ralph.* 1977. Honey.